Place in story-time

Geography through stories at key stages 1 and 2 (revised edition)

Heather Norris Nicholson

Series editor: Margaret Smeaton

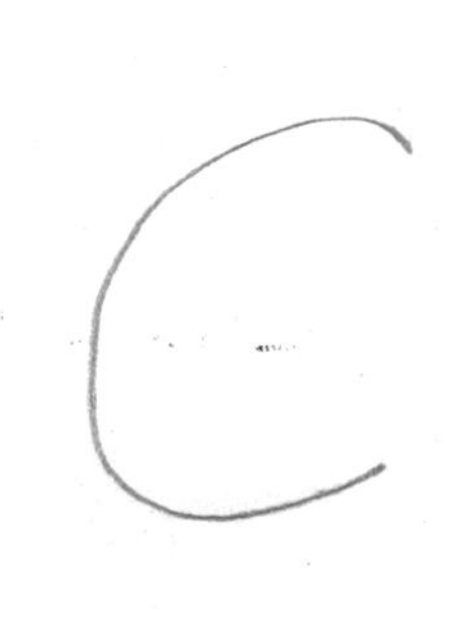

Foreword

In the mid-1930s, the author S.P.B. Mais gave a series of children's radio broadcasts which were later published in *Delight in books* (Mais 1938). It is a book which is still relevant and makes worthwhile reading today. Mais points out that through books one can learn much about other people's lives and other places and enjoy the wildest of adventures without the discomforts and expense of actually travelling.

Television and easier modes of travel today make more claims on children's lives and give them a wider visual insight into the world beyond their home environment. Nevertheless learning to read and use books is still a central educational requirement and learning about other people and different locations lies at the heart of geographical education in the primary school.

In this completely revised, updated and expanded edition of *Place in story-time* Heather Norris Nicholson presents many ideas about different kinds of stories and their relevance to the revised national curriculum, not only in regard to the teaching of geography but also in a cross-curricular approach. She gives many examples of children's books and suggests work in the classroom which can be linked to their study. The activities are comprehensive and the teacher could adapt them to any appropriate story.

Margaret Smeaton

Acknowledgements

The author is grateful to the many story-tellers and other experts who have shared their skills and insights with her. Special thanks are due to her students and also to teachers with whom she worked on in-service courses in Leeds, West Yorkshire. Thanks also to Sally and Richard Greenhill for the photograph used on the front cover and Margaret Smeaton for the photograph on page 4. Sonia Benster at The Children's Bookshop, Huddersfield also deserves particular mention for helping with the revision of the text in 1996.

ISBN 1 899085 21 1
First published 1994
First revised edition 1996
Impression number 10 9 8 7 6 5 4 3 2
Year 2001 2000 1999 1998

Published by the Geographical Association, 160 Solly Street, Sheffield S1 4BF. The Geographical Association is a registered charity: no 313129. The Publications Officer of the GA would be happy to hear from other potential a contact the Officer via the GA at the address above. e author and do not necessarily represent those of the

Editing: White Line
Design: Chris Hand
Printed and bound in

Contents

Foreword *page 2*

Introduction *page 4*

Stories in the school curriculum *page 5*

Sources of stories *page 9*

Working with stories *page 12*

Activities *page 14*

Examples of using published stories *page 21*

Appendix 1: Information sources for children's books *page 37*

Appendix 2: Bibliography *page 38*

Introduction

Approaching geography through story is one means of developing children's world view. Stories help to foster children's curiosity about their own changing world, and furnish images which help children to make sense of the complexities and contradictions which surround them and also to connect the present to the past and the future. Stories may help to confront stereotyping, to reinforce new understandings and to extend children's geographical experience. They therefore have considerable value with all ability ranges, and particular relevance for children with special needs.

Many children first meet the diversity of different people's outlooks on the world through stories. Later, awareness of other perspectives comes through school links with children elsewhere and through talking with adults in school and outside it. Primary geography offers scope for exploring how people give different meanings to places and hold a variety of viewpoints. Different perspectives in geographical stories stimulate children's thinking and can validate their own experiences. Stories can help children to identify and interpret information, sift fact from fiction, solve problems and make decisions.

Other people's stories may help children to see how the inner and outer worlds of experience inter-relate. If their role as listeners to other people's stories and other points of view can bring new awareness and meaning, perhaps the children can also become storytellers and help to promote a sense of understanding, appreciation and responsibility for the places and people around them. As teachers of geography, we have a rich resource to draw upon which should enable the children we teach to become a new generation of storytellers with very important stories to tell.

Stories in the school curriculum

Opportunities to use stories in the curriculum can be found, with a little ingenuity, in all aspects of school work. Assemblies, fieldwork, practical work and classroom work can all explore the richness of stories. In particular, stories can be a powerful means of forging links between different subjects in the curriculum.

Stories in the geography curriculum

Stories from whatever source provide an exciting start for geographical activity. Whether news reports, eye-witness accounts or fiction, reading aloud or re-telling a story can kindle imaginative thinking. Care is needed in initiating such an approach. No story should be overworked. Suggested activities on pages 14 to 20 focus on using stories both in specific geographical ways and in cross-curricular teaching. These ideas should be seen as a springboard from which teachers, according to their experience, interests and circumstances, can explore further possibilities.

Stories can supplement other geographical resources to help children visualise different places and lifestyles, and to acquire informed understanding about people's ways of life in different parts of the world. They offer children windows upon other worlds beyond their own.

Stories need not be confined to story-time! Sometimes they can be used as a source of geographical information to set alongside fieldwork or classroom activities such as mapping, using artefacts or compiling a database. They help to introduce young children to people, places and ideas, and can be supplemented by using other materials and by contact with real people.

National curriculum requirements

Stories can contribute to fulfilling many requirements of the revised geography national curriculum. In particular, they can be relevant to different parts of the Programmes of Study at key stages 1 and 2 (as shown in the table overleaf). The activity numbers in the second column of the table refer to the activities described on pages 14 to 20. Stories lend themselves readily to the development of geographical skills, the study of places and thematic enquiry. They provide an ideal context for asking geographical questions in ways which build upon younger children's practical exploration of their immediate surroundings and extend their geographical awareness. At key stage 2, stories complement other geographical approaches as they provide varied contexts and settings in which investigation may occur.

In short, the revised Order for geography with its renewed emphasis upon investigative approaches, thematic study and locality studies gives a strong signal for the continuing importance of developing pupils' understanding of place through stories.

Description	Activity numbers (pages 14-20)
Skills	
follow directions	9, 11, 12, 13, 14
observe and talk about a familiar place	13
use geographical vocabulary to talk about places	1, 2, 5-9, 12, 13, 15-22
make a representation of a real or imaginary place	2, 4, 6, 8, 15
follow a route using a plan	8, 9, 11, 12
identify familiar features on photographs and pictures	1, 5, 6, 8, 13
make a map of a short route, showing features in the correct order	8, 9, 15
use the index and contents pages to find information in an atlas	12, 15, 16, 25, 26
draw a sketch map using symbols and a key	8
Knowledge and understanding of places	
name familiar features of the local area	7, 22
identify activities carried out by people in the local area	18
demonstrate an awareness of the world beyond their local area	1-3, 5-8, 12-21, 22, 23-26
name the country in which they live	16
describe uses of land and buildings in the local area	22
identify features of a locality outside the local area and suggest how these might affect the lives of the people who live there	5, 17, 18, 20
describe similarities and differences between the local area and another locality specified in the programme of study	5, 13, 15, 18
use correct geographical vocabulary to identify types of landscape features and activities with which they are familiar in the local area	15
compare features and occupations of the local area with the other localities specific in the programme of study	20
describe how the landscape of an area outside the local area has been changed by human actions	23
give an accout of a recent or proposed change in a locality	22
describe how the daily life of a locality in an economically developing country is affected by its landscape, weather and wealth	20
Physical geography	
describe contrasting weather conditions in parts of the world	14
identify and describe a familiar landscape feature	5, 6, 7

Human geography	
recognise that buildings are used for different purposes	18
describe ways in which people make journeys	8, 9, 10, 12-15
recognise that adults do different kinds of work	18, 19-21
give reasons why people make journeys of different lengths	8, 10, 12, 14, 15
identify how goods and services needed in the local community are provided	18, 22
give reasons why people change their homes	22, 24
explain why different forms of transport are used	12
explain why few people live in some areas and many people live in others	17
Environmental geography	
express personal likes and dislikes about features of the local area	17, 22
describe ways in which people have changed the environment	22, 23, 24
suggest how they could improve the quality of their own environment	22, 23
describe an activity designed to improve the local environment or a place they have visited	22, 23
discuss whether some types of environment need special protection	22, 23, 24

Cross-subject links

Stories with a strong geographical bias may provide a means of fulfilling other national curriculum requirements too. As primary teachers have responsibility for the whole curriculum, they are ideally placed to identify areas of overlap in which they can use resources and curriculum time effectively (CCW 1991). Forging appropriate curriculum links requires teachers to identify links with other subjects and cross-curricular elements (Hughes and Marsden 1995).

English and history
Stories which inform about geography can also help fulfil the requirements for English in the National Curriculum. Varied approaches to geography teaching, including the use of stories, provide opportunities for the development of language skills such as speaking, listening, reading and writing (CCW 1991).

Interviewing skills and the handling of primary and secondary sources are integral to much of the enquiry-based learning on which primary geography depends. Role-play and improvisation involve children in problem-solving, decision-making and understanding different points of view as they develop responses to the places, characters and situations encountered in different stories. Interviewing characters from fiction, devising episodes not described in a story, creating alternative endings, setting a narrative in other localities, and retelling tales for another audience, are other possibilities. Through such means, children can thus become closely involved with the people, places and predicaments which a story may embrace. Tales which indicate how places and communities change over time provide a clear link with history.

Mathematics
As geography and mathematics share many key concepts, a story centred on a journey might invite work on aspects such as distance, direction, networks and scale. Stories with a sense of place could prompt number work on area, size and density of population.

Science, technology and design
Writing on contemporary environmental issues might prompt scientific investigations that complement the story's perspective on the relationship between people and their surroundings. Alternatively, practical response to details in fiction could provide scope for technology and design-related activities.

Art
Children can be encouraged to make their own drawings and paintings to illustrate their own stories and published stories. They can also write their own stories to accompany artists' scenes of places and people.

Music and dance
Music's capacity to express ideas, thoughts and feelings offers important stimuli for children's geographical understanding and imagination. Children can be introduced to stories already set to music, e.g. Prokofiev's 'Peter and the Wolf'. An awareness of traditional or modern music and lyrics can invoke a sense of place. Dance provides an alternative vocabulary of movement, gesture and rhythm, through which children may respond to aspects of their own surroundings and other places encountered through stories (Norris Nicholson 1993, Chapter 11).

Cross-curricular elements
Since stories play a crucial role in children's overall development at primary level, they touch upon many experiences and strands of understanding which are cross-curricular in nature. All contribute to a balanced curriculum within each school's individual vision of the purpose and scope of education. The following table suggests how stories can contribute to cross-curricular elements in various ways.

Contribution of stories to cross-curricular elements	
Geography for all	Stories help to broaden children's understanding of and respect for others. Through stories, all children can explore issues such as equal opportunities, special needs and life in a multicultural society.
Transferable skills	Stories can help children to develop many core skills which are transferable across the whole curriculum: communication, numeracy, problem-solving and the use of information technology.
Social and environmental themes	Many stories with a geographical flavour contribute to children's understanding of and participation in the world around them. Three themes have become pre-eminent: children's appreciation of the environment, the economy (including industry and the world of work), and the well-being of society.

Sources of stories

Stories of many kinds occur in daily life. We can help children to recognise their wide variety and the differences between them. Whether fictional, factual or anecdotal, stories may share certain elements but may also be very different in length, mood, style and message. Some stories remain unchanging, while others, such as news stories, develop as material is added and as shifts of emphasis and new interpretations occur. Some are short-lived and have importance mainly for the teller, while others last thousands of years and hold meaning for many people.

The table gives some examples of types of story and some of the ways in which they can be classified. What other characteristics could you look for?

Type of story	Form	Mode	Other characteristics
Folk tale	Verbal/written	Fictional	Long-lived Widespread Culturally rooted Slowly changing
News story	Written/ broadcast	Factual	Short-lived Widespread Rapidly changing
Novel or short story	Written	Fictional	Medium duration Unchanging
Personal account	Verbal/written	Factual/ anecdotal	Short-lived Communicated to only a few
Sacred story	Verbal/ written/ retold	Myth/ historical	Long-lived Widespread Culturally rooted Unchanging in essentials
Travel story	Written	Factual/ anecdotal	Medium duration Unchanging
Bedtime story	Verbal	Fictional	Very short-lived Not normally recorded

Personal stories

Personal stories can express a child's own world of experiences, perceptions and interpretations. Children can learn to observe and use their senses to gain first-hand knowledge from which they can create their own stories — or compare fiction critically with their own experience. Imaginary stories about known places are lively starting points for developing awareness and language skills.

The many published examples, e.g. C.S. Lewis' *The lion, the witch and the wardrobe*, Laurie Lee's *Cider with Rosie* or Dannie Abse's *There was a young man from Cardiff*, of childhood memories about places offer opportunities to compare real localities with the imaginary as well as providing stimulus for further imaginative work. A child's geographical imagination thus builds on knowledge and understanding drawn from other sources. Such activities mean that pupils can apply real facts to imaginary contexts with understanding, and yet learn to distinguish fact from fiction, e.g. Ivan Southall's *Ash Road* — a fictitious story about a bush fire.

Personal stories about living, working and growing up in an area may also foster children's sense of place and help them to identify with particular settings through recognition and familiarity, e.g. Floella Benjamin's *Coming to England* — a strongly autobiographical story about leaving Trinidad. The records of other people's experiences may show how localities, communities and ways of life change, and reveal that different people may view the same places very differently, e.g. Jill Paton Walsh's *Babylon* — an urban story resonant with issues of how places and communities change over time.

Stories collected through visits and interviews in the community can be compared with pictures and accounts of different localities or of the same place at other periods in time. Recording other people's oral accounts in writing or on maps, or using them in practical creative work, are some of the ways in which this readily available but under-used resource can enrich geographical learning.

Publicised current stories

From an early age, children are exposed to stories which become well publicised through the media. Printed and broadcast factual accounts about unusual or familiar places and people bombard us with images and influence how we interpret and make sense of the complex world around us. Children's news programmes, schools broadcasts and documentaries extend children's mental maps of places, issues and lifestyles far beyond their direct experience. Current events are also familiar elements of school assemblies, where they often share with geography our concern for fostering a better understanding about living in an interdependent world.

Published diaries, explorers' logs and travellers' tales likewise bring personal experience to public attention and may similarly raise issues of motive and interpretation. They also present opportunities for atlas work and investigations into lifestyle, landscape and locality (Kingsley 1993).

Some public stories begin as private matters: they may be based on personal experience yet gain publicity through the media. With older children, teachers might explore such issues as privacy, the public right to know, and other questions demanding critical thinking.

Traditional stories and folk tales

Story-telling is part of an oral tradition which has, in many places, gradually lost its significance. Many examples of this oral tradition survive, although it is threatened by changing patterns of family and community life such as the increasing interaction between peoples and the ever-expanding presence of instant global communications. Many folk stories now exist only in printed form as a result of deliberate attempts to collect and record them, but in the process many changes have occurred to the original tales.

Traditional tales and legends may give a valuable yet selective view of another part of the world. Through these tales children can be made aware of how places, people and stories change over time (e.g. Kirollos 1981; Gavin 1989; Appiah 1987; French 1994).

Ideally traditional tales, in whatever form, should complement modern stories (see Appendix 2). Opportunities to visit other countries or to invite visitors from other regions may also provide a means of building up a school collection of stories about distant localities (see Activity 26 on page 20).

Stories in other forms

Stories exist in many other forms too, but all may lend themselves to geographical activity if viewed with a resourceful eye and an ingenious mind. From epic film to nursery rhyme or limerick, stories are captured in image and word in every age and in all places. Ancient pictographs and rock paintings illustrate tales from long ago. The Bayeux and D-Day tapestries tell stories in a historical and geographical context. Advertisements, cartoons and news headlines offer a diet of ever-changing stories. Some kind of story line underpins operas and musicals, and may be present in dance performances and choral works. There will never be a shortage of stories to choose from.

Working with stories

Choosing stories

Many children's stories are set within places, either real or imaginary, and in different periods. This may seem obvious, but the way in which a story deals with *place* and *time* is basic to its value in geography.

Stories, then, are useful if they have a strong sense of place or if they show how places, people and points of view change through time. Geographical vocabulary may help to set the scene, or to describe activities or people–place relationships. Words and pictures may provide a basis for comparison between the direct experience of *here* and *now* and the imagined reality of *there* and *then*. Some stories powerfully evoke a sense of a locality in or beyond the local area and offer insights into distant places, lifestyles and circumstances.

In a story, distinctive landscapes or settlements may have clearly defined layouts through which the characters move and interact. How can you make use of these spatial aspects of a story? Perhaps the setting can be modelled or mapped, or compared with a more familiar setting. You can also consider the living arrangements of the characters, and their attitudes and ways of behaving.

Hidden dimensions in stories

Many stories have hidden dimensions which go unnoticed if we concentrate only on the narrative itself. Such stories gain in meaning if you set them in a wider context. For example, it may be useful to find out where a story came from, how it reached us and how its meaning may have changed in the process. If this information is not readily available, it may be necessary to make informed guesses. Sometimes the story itself may give a clue, as may the biographical details of the author, if known (e.g. Grifalconi 1986).

If you know the original context in which a story — especially a traditional one — was first told, you can use pictures, artefacts and sound effects to set the contemporary scene, and so to help the children interpret the story and respond to it. Traditional stories often come from a social and cultural context very different from our own. Encourage the children to ask and answer brief questions:

- **Who would have told the story originally?**
- **How?**
- **Where?**
- **Why?**

It is often tempting to gloss over difficulties of translation and interpretation, and of the evolution of the story into its recorded form, but these questions may throw light on how to understand the story today.

Stories sometimes share common elements even if they originated many miles apart. You can discuss with the children possible reasons for these similarities. Ask them to suggest how similar responses might arise in different situations — for instance, to meet basic needs of shelter and subsistence, or to form part of a celebration or a ceremony. This will help them to appreciate elements of shared experience, as well as diversity, in contrasting settings.

As traditional stories spread from their point of origin, they often change as they travel. You can explore this process, and ask the children to suggest future destinations for certain stories as they continue to spread through the movement of people and through global communications. How would these stories be likely to change and develop?

The cultural facet is only one of the hidden dimensions of stories. Another useful facet to explore is that of the many people who are involved in bringing a published story to its readership — author, editor, illustrator, publisher and bookseller. If you invite such people into the classroom, the children can ask them about the hidden lives and livelihoods behind the stories. An author of children's stories, for example, could foster the children's awareness of how they themselves draft, revise and develop their own written work (Chapple, 1989). How do writers think of ideas and develop them? How do they manage their time, collaborate with illustrators, develop their own style? It is important to choose such speakers with care: they must be accustomed to speaking to young children and relate well to them.

Exchanging stories

Class links with another school could lead to a sharing of children's own stories as part of a wider geographical focus on another locality. Links between schools in English-speaking countries would be particularly appropriate for younger children. At key stage 2 an exchange of short stories or picture books with a school overseas might well require help with translation and cooperation with language teachers. As with any linking scheme, schools exchanging stories have to be both sensitive and realistic in their expectations of what any class is able to offer.

Activities

Introduction

All the following activities encourage the development of geographical language skills and understanding through story-related work. Where possible, they are grouped into broad themes.

At the teacher's discretion, they can be adapted for work with the whole-class, small groups and individuals.

The time taken will depend on the extent of follow-up activity and on the character of the story. Activities may be contained within a single session or developed as part of a half-term theme.

Suitable stories with geographical interest are listed in Appendix 2. Supplementary pictures, maps, writing and drawing materials can be accumulated over time. Programmable toys, computers, cameras or compasses are required in some activities.

Pictures and sounds

1 Stories in pictures

Discuss with the children how to retell a story using pictures. Discuss where the people, creatures or objects are and what activities are taking place. Ask them to look out for geographical features and for clues which suggest links and movement between different parts of the story. Introduce geographical terms wherever appropriate.

2 Out-of-sight stories

Discuss with the children which scenes have pictures. Ask them to look for hidden parts of a picture-story. What might be hidden from view? Who or what else might be in the picture? How might other scenes in the story be illustrated? How might the final scene be shown pictorially if the *last page of text* were missing?

3 Sound in stories

Ask the children to imagine what kinds of sounds they might hear in the places mentioned in a story. They could record or improvise a sound-track for the story which captures the sense of place. Ask the children if any other senses might be used in responding to the story.

4 Models and stage sets for stories

Plan the setting of the story using a floor mat, or draw your own outline plan to represent the setting. Use card, boxes and paper to model the features of the story. Ask the children to act out the story using puppets and a script, or ask them to act out parts of the story using suitable background settings.

5 Story settings

Discuss with the children any clues about the setting of the story. Ask if they think it is set in a real place. Can they find other pictures of that place? Ask them to compare their pictures with those in the story and spot any differences. If the story is set in an imaginary place, ask the children to find pictures of real places which match the story, at least in part. Discuss how the writer or illustrator might disguise a real place or reveal clues about where the story is set. The children might make a word list which identifies similarities and differences between a place in a story and somewhere they know.

Story locations

6 Stories on location

Ask the children to imagine they are a film crew. Their brief is to transfer a story to another location. Ask them to devise a storyboard, and then to make pictures or take photographs to retell the story in a place they know. The pictures and text can be sequenced together and captions printed using the computer. Discuss how they might tell their story to someone who could not see the pictures.

7 Placing a story

Ask the children to retell a story in their own words. Encourage them to find pictures to illustrate it and to locate any places mentioned using a map. Discuss how the story might be relocated in an area they know, and ask them to include details as clues to its new setting.

Journeys

8 Story journeys

Some stories include a clearly defined journey which can be drawn on paper to show how different features and places are visited in turn. Discuss how the setting of a story might be shown on a piece of paper using pictures or symbols to indicate where the characters go. Ask the children to map any routes described in the story. What do characters visit or pass by on the journey? Could they go anywhere else?

Discuss how the story might end differently if they took another route. Might the story change if another character went too? Would other travellers follow the same route, stop in different places or travel at a different speed?

9 Marking the way

Using a story with a journey, ask the children to trace the route out on a large sheet of paper and decide where to place a limited number of signposts or clues to mark the route. Ask them how they might mark their route in code or in other ways without spoiling the place for others.

10 Journey questionnaires

Ask the children to work out the route of a journey described in a story and then to devise questions for an interview with either the character or another reader. They should check that their questions can be answered before trying them on others! Other children can answer the journey questionnaire in role as characters. A sample questionnaire is given in the table.

A JOURNEY QUESTIONNAIRE NAME	DATE . . . .
Title of story	
Name of character	
Where did your journey start?	
What is the reason for your journey?	
How did you travel?	
What have you visited or passed by on the way?	
How long did your journey take?	
Where did your journey end?	
How far did you travel?	
What else would you like to add?	

11 Stories and programmable toys

Ask the children to devise a series of commands which match the route of a simple journey in a story. Encourage them to give instructions which control straight-line distances, moves and turns. Ask them to type in their commands, using a programmable toy that draws a line as it moves. Ask them to check that their programming matches the actual route followed by a character in the story. Encourage them to model other parts of the story's setting using cardboard boxes or floor apparatus for the programmable toy to negotiate.

12 Locating the action

Ask the children to locate places in the story on a map or globe. Discuss with them how people might travel to these places in different ways and along different routes — shortest, most scenic, cheapest, and so on. Ask them to identify the direction they would travel in at different stages of their journey.

13 Travellers' tales

Discuss how travellers may describe a journey or a place in a story from different points of view. Ask the children to suggest which details in a story might be perceived or described differently by different characters. Ask them to suggest different versions of journeys or visits in their own locality, and to suggest possible reasons for the differences. Encourage them to compare any setting or journey in a story with a familiar journey of their own, concentrating on what they would see.

14 Packing their bags

Discuss with the children what they might take with them if they were to visit somewhere in a story or to make a similar journey. Ask them what things they would need to take with them. Suggest that they keep a journal during their travels and record what they experience. They might also devise travel logs for characters who make journeys in stories.

15 Story postbag

Ask the children to address a postcard to someone at a place in a story. Discuss how the card might travel, and ask them to plot its route and to investigate how long the journey might take. Alternatively, suggest that the children might imagine sending a postcard from where the story is set. Ask them to design a suitable postcard and write a message on the back about what the place is like.

16 Stories on the move

Discuss with the children how a story might travel to the classroom from where it is first written or told. Ask the children to locate the story, and its writer and illustrator, on a map. Ask them to retell the journey of their story arriving in the classroom in a series of pictures or a travel diary. The children might tell the story from the manuscript's point of view, from the earliest stages as ideas in the author's notebook through to the printed book arriving at the school. The journey might include such mishaps as almost falling overboard, going through a machine wash or getting lost in the post.

Lifestyles

17 Stepping into stories

Help the children to imagine themselves into a story through discussion or drama. Ask them what they might enjoy most or least about being in places mentioned in the story. Encourage them to think about what they might miss most about their present lifestyle if suddenly transported to the setting of the story.

18 All in a day

Discuss with children how a character in a story might spend a whole day. Ask them to devise a log which shows what the character might do at certain times in the story, and add in additional detail for other times. Encourage the children to record where their characters might go, what they might do, whom they might meet, and so on. Ask them to compare this routine with their own lifestyle.

19 Story lines

Ask the children to write a letter or diary entry which reflects the hobbies or interests of one character in a story. They might also turn a memorable occasion from a story into a newspaper article or into a short scripted radio interview or broadcast, using evidence from the story and elsewhere to build up a sense of place and event.

20 This is your life

Ask the children to decide which character from a story they would most like to interview for a television programme. Discuss with them what questions they might ask and how they could find out more about the lifestyle and home of their chosen character.

21 Lifelines

Discuss with the children how characters might have had other experiences in life which influence what they do in the story. Ask them to devise a biography of their chosen character from birth to the time when the story takes place. Encourage them to project their character's life into the future using evidence from the story and elsewhere. Alternatively, ask them to interview their character about his/her life so far and hopes for the future.

The environment

22 Ten ways to the future

Discuss with the class what to include in a list of ten ways to improve the local area. Encourage them to recognise how opinions vary. Ask them to suggest a set of ten principles by which a favourite character might try to improve the world or the setting of the story. Discuss how characters might hope for and bring about different types of change. Ask the children what their own priorities might be in making where they live a better place. Encourage them to identify any difficulties they might meet in bringing about these changes. The children could present their ideas orally as part of a debate, public meeting or studio interview, or in writing.

Factual stories

23 Newsdesk

Discuss with the children recent news stories, and find examples of different kinds of stories. Environmental issues such as pollution, land-use, traffic or farming may provide starting points for research into conflicting interests which the children could develop as a script, through role-play, through public debate, or in writing. Ask them to identify and account for different points of view. Devise a role-play in which the children take different perspectives and debate the issues. Do their ideas match those in the story? Monitor the news for eco-stories and mark them on a wall map. Social issues may prompt follow-up work in similar ways according to the age and character of the class. The children can supplement their stories with details from other sources.

24 Disasters

When stories feature disasters and accidents, discuss with the children how people may behave differently in response to events such as hurricanes, floods, earthquakes, forest fires, avalanches or drought. Ask them how they might plan a rescue operation to help people, creatures or places threatened by natural forces or other dangers. Discuss with the class how emergency equipment and relief supplies can help in times of disasters. Discuss what supplies would be needed in different types of emergency. Encourage them to think about how different people work together when disaster strikes, and how some countries try to prepare for, or prevent, emergencies. Ask them to design a poster or write a news report with the title 'Quick Action Saves Lives'. Encourage them to create the stories of people involved in the disaster as rescue workers or victims.

Collecting stories

25 A story database

Discuss with the class how stories may come from or be set in different places. Ask them to make a survey of stories to find out where they come from and mark the information on a wall map with coloured stickers or pins. Create a database so that the children can graph their findings. Discuss possible reasons for stories coming from particular places.

26 An A to Z of stories

Discuss with the children how they could compile an A to Z of stories from around the world. Ask them to make an alphabetical list of countries so that they can match a story with each country. The children might design a questionnaire for use with a local library, bookshop or other organisations so that they can gather information about different stories. The results could be used to create an international story festival for the whole school or a resource list for local schools. Encourage the children to map the titles onto a wall map. Children could make book reviews for stories selected from the A to Z. A class could also gather this information about their own reading over a term or longer and record it each time they met a new story in school or elsewhere.

Examples of using published stories

Not so fast, Songololo! (Daly 1987)

Geography

- Discuss where the story is set
- Find South Africa on the globe and on maps
- Map the journey described in the story
- Sequence the places passed on the journey
- Compare it with a shopping journey in the home locality
- Compare details about people, places and traffic passed
- Visit a shoe shop and interview the shop manager
- Map the 'life journey' of a shoe
- Look at other currencies
- Visit a bank
- Write to the South African National Tourist Board and make a display
- Plan journeys with other people — older, younger, etc.
- Design better access for people with special needs

History

- Make a family tree
- Collect photographs and artefacts
- Make a time-line for child, parents and grandparents
- Compare where different people go shopping — now and then
- Compare shops and shopping — now and then
- Compare footwear — now and then
- Chart changing shoe sizes
- Compare the cost of shoes — now and then
- Look at pre-decimal money
- Interview grandparents about when they were young
- Compare with *The Elves and the Shoemaker*
- Use artefacts, including a shoemaker's last

Language

- Discussion
- Write additional scenes and dialogue
- Devise a script for conversations at a bus stop
- Read
- Send letters for more information

Science

- Design footwear
- Test the strengths of materials
- Use recycling materials — e.g. sandals made from rubber tyres

Maths

- Use money — shopping, fares, etc.

- Count the number of people passed on the way
- Count numbers of buses, cars, shops, etc.
- Measure the time taken to walk or run at different speeds
- Measure the length of your own feet

A balloon for Granddad (Gray and Ray 1991)

Geography

- Direction work — up, across, over, etc.
- Use a compass
- Survey people moving from place to place and their reasons for doing so
- Survey types of travel and routes
- Compare lifestyles in different places
- Discuss what settling into a new place is like
- Invite a visitor to share experiences
- Compare different landscapes — desert, island, mountain, etc.
- Compare climates
- Compare houses and buildings with those in the local area
- Match artists' pictures to real photographs and compare them
- Locate the route of the balloon on a globe
- Make a family tree and link it to a map
- Record wind and wind direction at school
- Survey windy and sheltered places around school
- Design sheltered places for the playground

History

- Record experiences of older people
- Compare life — now and then
- Collect memories of moving house and coming to another country
- Compare life in desert areas — now and then (Ancient Egypt)

Science

- Compare different types of flight — balloon, bird, etc.
- Compare building structures and materials
- Test construction methods
- Design a weather vane
- Compare food and diet

Art

- Use patterns and shapes
- Compare decoration in different countries
- Design a building
- Look at colour in different landscapes

Language

- Descriptive writing about the flight of a balloon
- Keep a travel diary of things visited or passed by

- Imaginative writing about emigration and moving house
- Release a balloon with a message
- Prepare a script for a 'balloon debate'

Religious education

Discussion to cover:

- Coming to terms with disappointment
- Valuing the memories of other people
- Making connections with people elsewhere
- Understanding other people's lifestyles

Can't catch me (Prater 1993)

Geography

- Compare town and country
- Contrast land-use and landscape
- Meet people in different occupations
- Look at landscapes and activities in different seasons
- Draw a map of a circular journey
- Sequence the places and events in the story
- Retell the story using pictures and a map
- Survey the occupations of people in the school and the community
- Using colour and symbols, record the land-use in the vicinity of the school

Language

- Devise a tourist leaflet for the journey
- Send postcards during the journey
- Creative writing about travel, places visited, etc.
- Descriptive writing about changing seasons
- Interview people with different occupations
- Keep a travel journal
- Compare with an actual journey or holiday

History

- Make a time-line for oneself
- Collect photographs of self and surroundings showing change
- Compare town and country — then and now
- Compare occupations — then and now
- Ask older people for their recollections

Art

- Explore colour and seasonal change
- Look for colours in the landscape
- Record patterns in surroundings
- Make a photographic record of school
- Make a pipe-cleaner sculpture of old farm machinery

- Claywork using textures from nature and machines

Science

- Test for heat and seasonal change
- Record process of growth and ageing

Grandma's pictures (Hughes 1993)

Geography

- Map Uncle Will's route to school
- Map the children's routes to school
- Compare landmarks, people, sounds, etc., en route
- Locate Australia on maps and plan a route to get there
- Survey people's mobility in school and their reasons for migration
- Compare lifestyles and landscapes in Australia with those in the home area
- Compare different regions of Australia
- Compare Will's experiences with today
- Compare Will's life with Aboriginal lifestyles

History

- Record how people grow and change
- Make a family tree or time-line
- Interview older people
- Compare places through time
- Compare Will's experiences with today
- Compare school life — then and now
- Visit an older school or plan a Victorian school day
- Role-play experiences of new settlers to Australia
- Compare toys and games — then and now
- Interpret photographs and compare cameras — then and now
- Build a class museum with loaned possessions

Language

- Write diaries, letters, the ship's log, etc.
- Describe the travel conditions and the life of the early settlers — this can be improvised
- Devise characters and interviews
- Record memories

Descriptive writing

- Make immigration leaflets for new arrivals
- Read Aboriginal legends
- Invent a meeting with Aboriginal people
- Read extracts from *Walkabout* (Marshall 1979) and *Tin Lizzie and little Nell* (Spier 1990)

Art

- Design emigration campaign posters
- Make a model of school — past and present
- Design school uniforms
- Work with light-sensitive paper — see Colledge (1984) for myriad suggestions
- Look at the patterns and colours in the Australian landscape
- Make a sand painting

When we went to the park (Hughes 1985)

Geography

- Make a visit to the local park
- Plan the route
- Take photographs, recording information, etc.
- Draw the route and include places passed on the way in their correct order
- Survey people, buildings, traffic, etc., passed on the way
- Interview people in the park
- Survey activities in the park
- Plan visits in other seasons
- List appropriate clothing for different weather conditions
- Map other places visited in the local area
- Map safe and unsafe places in the local area
- Look for ways to make the local area safer
- Use directions
- Survey litter and eyesores
- Invite a local planner to school

History

- Compare the park — then and now
- Compare people's clothes, games and toys — then and now
- Look for clues about changes in the locality
- Record seasonal changes
- Make a time-line for the park or local area
- Collect photographs of the local area
- Collect photographs and paintings of past 'days out'
- Devise dance and movement to suitable music for summer outings
- Have a Victorian or 1960s (Teddy bears') picnic in the park using costumes, old recipes and games, etc.

Art

- Make rubbings, patterns or nature sculpture from found materials
- Make a collage of buildings and street scenes
- Paint park scenes
- Look at paintings of parks by, for example, Emily Carr, Mary Cassat, Frida Kahlo, L.S. Lowry, Seurat, Georgia O'Keefe, Pissaro, and experiment with painting in different ways

Maths

- Plan a route, working out distance, direction, etc.
- Plan a timetable for the visit
- Sort and count observations on the visit
- Look at the numbering of houses on the way
- Compare size and scale — near/far, large/small, high/low

Language

- Descriptive and creative writing about the visit
- Interview people: 'As I was going to St Ives'
- Design a tourist leaflet for the park or a local trail guide
- Role-play in the park — asking directions, finding something, sitting on a park bench, meeting someone, etc.

The farmer's gift (Harbott and Harbott 1990)

Geography

- Locate the country on the map
- Compare its lifestyle, landscape and houses with those of the local area
- Visit local shops and compare fruits and vegetables in both localities
- Taste mango and other fruits and vegetables as appropriate
- Compare rural and urban lifestyles
- Compare images of rich and poor in modern India and the UK
- Write to the Indian National Tourist Office and plan an imaginary journey
- Invite a visitor who has lived in or visited India

History

- Compare old and new buildings in both countries using pictures
- Compare the palace in the story with a real palace (tourist information)
- Compare life in the past in rural and urban areas
- Compare different reasons for British links with India

Science

- Test how to preserve food in different climates
- Bake clay tablets in an oven
- Make part of an Indian meal and compare Indian and British diets
- Filter water using different materials
- Compare health conditions in India with those in the local area
- Research insects and reptiles in both countries
- Make dyes from natural materials

Language

- Creative and descriptive writing about the place and characters in the story
- Devise additional scenes and improvise dialogue for them
- Compare the written languages and try to identify the characters of an Indian language

- Read or retell extracts from other writings in English and Indian stories (e.g. *Mahabharata* — an epic traditional Indian story)

Art

- Paint subtropical fruits and vegetables
- Design decorations for an urban rickshaw
- Try hand-painting using traditional designs
- Make designs for a palace, and for rural home interiors, using the picture
- Try block-printing and other forms of printing
- Try enlarging a Mughal painting
- Make a casket for a precious possession

The quilt (Jonas 1992)

Geography

- Map landscapes of the quilt
- Label the landscapes — hills, woodland, river etc.
- Compare different landscape features
- Relate the landscape patchwork to real landscapes
- Mark on a map where 'quilt landscapes' exist
- Practise giving directions
- Devise clues in a search for something
- Match animals to different parts of the world
- Contrast life in the wild and circus life
- Identify features on aerial photographs and oblique views
- Devise a grid reference system for the quilt, and devise a quiz based on this
- Work on journeys and directions
- Compare climates in different parts of the world

History

- Compare beds and bedclothes through time and one's own life
- Compare old and new possessions using artefacts and photographs
- Compare birthdays and special occasions
- Compare old and new toys and books
- Compare ways of keeping warm through time
- Trace the life story of a piece of coal
- Make a time-line or personal history
- Interview older people
- Make a memory box

Maths

- Calculate ages in family and in class
- Practise telling the time
- Work with tessellations and shapes
- Use grid co-ordinates for the patchwork quilt

Science

- Test different materials for thickness, etc.
- Look for evidence of camouflage in the animal world
- Test objects which float and sink
- Grow mushrooms, or search for different kinds of fungus
- Test sight and visibility in different degrees of light and darkness
- Test reflective surfaces in the dark

Language

- Creative writing about dreams and nightmares
- Write about likes and dislikes
- Discuss equal opportunities and related feelings
- Using drama, improvise visits to different places
- Build characters through drama and role-play

Art

- Design and decorate a memory box
- Make a quilt in fabric or other materials
- Design different patterns for fabric printing

Katie Morag and the tiresome teddy (Hedderwick 1989)

Geography

- Look for islands on maps and the globe
- Survey the children to find whether they have been to any islands
- Locate the Hebridean island in the story
- Make model islands
- Identify island features in pictures and text
- Compare the island with the home area
- Compare the island with other islands that the children may have visited
- Compare housing styles and colours of the landscape with those of the local area
- Measure the distance from your locality to the nearest seaside and the nearest island
- Plan routes to the seaside
- Compare 'seaside experiences' of the class
- Identify features of seaside settings
- Make a rock-pool or tidal frieze with labels
- Research how tides occur
- Contrast the sea as a place for work and for play
- Discuss whether the seaside is a clean or a dirty place
- Practise directions at sea — port and starboard
- Use a compass
- Compare journeys to visit other family members
- Devise a weather chart

Science

- Compare parts of the body and growth
- Discuss how to care for things
- Investigate rocks using a hand-lens
- Test objects for floating and sinking
- Make a litter survey, and compare with flotsam and jetsam
- Research sea birds and the effect of oil slicks on them
- Research wind power
- Test model boats with sails, using a hair dryer to simulate the wind
- Build electricity circuits for a model lighthouse

Language

- Creative and descriptive writing
- Newspaper reporting
- Write messages for bottles
- Practise semaphore
- Devise a safety code for being at the seaside
- Write to the Crofting Association, etc., for up-to-date information

History

- Make a family tree or time-line
- Compare landmarks and memories of different people
- Compare island life and life at sea — then and now
- Compare homes of grannies — then and now
- Retell stories associated with sea rescues and life at sea
- Research where people went to from the Scottish islands

Maths

- Measure distances and travel times to the sea
- Compare ages, heights and other measurements of those in the class
- Compare sea and land measurements, e.g. fathoms, knots
- Compare the size of a lifeboat or fishing boat with that of a car in the playground
- Plan provisions for a fishing voyage for the whole class

Over the green hills (Isadora 1992)

Geography

- Find the Transkei, Indian Ocean and South Africa on globes and maps
- Compare seashore with other seasides
- Compare homes, shops and village/neighbourhood within local vicinity
- Sequence places and features passed on the journey
- Map the journey described in the story
- Compare it with a journey to a friend or relation's home
- Discuss how people buy, sell and exchange in different places
- Compare seasons, and effects of seasonal change on daily lives
- Compare children's toys and games from different places — old and new

Language

- Compare with actual journey to visit family or friends
- Devise a conversation in the shop or with someone met on the journey
- Write poems using sounds of seasons, ocean, forest and village life
- Imagine a day in the life of someone passed on the journey
- Make a diary entry about being given something very special
- Devise a role-play about meeting someone with a problem
- Discuss why people tell stories and how home life might be without television
- Learn/devise 'campfire' or clapping songs

History

- Compare travelling to family and friends — now and then
- Compare lives and landscapes in the Transkei — now and then
- Collect memories of an older person
- Compare children's toys — old and new
- Identify how buildings change over time
- Compare lives with and without access to books and printed material

Science

- Test construction methods and materials
- Grow seeds under different conditions
- Compare plants and animals from different climates
- Compare fruits and vegetables from different climates

Art

- Compare artwork with other scenes of Transkei's farmlands and forests
- Look for colours and patterns in the Transkei and own surroundings
- Make prints on textiles, paper or clay
- Make pipe-cleaner models of vehicles

Maths

- Plan a route using directions, distances, etc.
- Design and measure a modelled scene from the story
- Sort and count observations from the journey
- Discuss other currencies and use money — shopping

Coming to England (Benjamin 1995)

Geography

- Locate all places mentioned in story using a globe and atlas
- Compare modern pictures of Trinidad and Britain
- Compare house styles and gardens in both capitals and in local area
- Discuss why people migrate — then and now
- Compare childhood and family life in Trinidad and UK
- Gather information about different aspects of Trinidad
- Compare carnivals and fairs in both countries

- Identify how ports and international travel have changed over time

History

- Discuss links between the Caribbean and Britain
- Find newspaper reports of arrivals of Caribbean immigrants in the 1950s
- Role-play recruiting jobs in the Caribbean and decision-making
- Find out about Black people living in British cities and society in earlier centuries
- Compare schools in Trinidad and local area — then and now

Language

- Keep a log of the journey to England
- Write about hopes and disappointments of moving elsewhere
- Discuss what it feels like to be inside/outside a group
- Compare how people behave towards strangers and each other
- Write about being made to feel invisible
- Imagine a sequel to the story
- Discuss how migration may divide and reunite families

Science

- Survey how electricity affects daily life
- Make a lighting circuit
- Experiment with buoyancy aids and discuss safety at sea
- Identify and make a display of plants used in health care and cooking
- Discuss tropical seasons, natural hazards and storm protection
- Compare flora and fauna in Britain and in Trinidad
- Chart weather reports for Caribbean and local area

Maths

- Compare currencies, time differences and the cost of telephone calls
- Measure and compare distances between places in the story
- Contact a removal or shipping company and work out the cost of moving house
- Use censuses or school records to identify patterns of movement of people
- Plan and cost a visit to the Caribbean using holiday brochures
- Survey land and house prices in two localities

Way home (Hathorn 1994)

Geography

- Map the route and sequence the places passed
- Identity best/worst aspects of city life
- Compare city in story with own local area
- Discuss hazards in town and country
- Compare buildings and a journey in local area with story's setting
- Map safe areas in own locality
- Talk about need for shelter and homes built of scrap materials

History

- Compare old and new building styles
- Compare old and new hazards in towns
- Compare lighting systems in cities — then and now

Language

- Discuss why animals are important to many people
- Survey attitudes towards animals and pets in the class
- Invite a speaker from the RSPCA
- Design a guide or poster about animal welfare
- Write about one day in the life of the child in the story
- Write a poem about loneliness and/or friendship
- Role-play a meeting with the boy

Art

- Make a frieze of a city by day and at night
- Retell the story using shadow puppets
- Model the boy's home using junk materials
- Make imaginary cities using different materials
- Design an 'ideal' city

Solo (Gergahty 1995)

Geography

- Locate Antarctica on globe and on maps
- Compare seasons and climate in polar regions with local area
- Discuss landscapes of ice, rock and water
- Identify lifeforms and human activity in Antarctica
- Plan an expedition to Antarctica and pack all survival items

History

- Talk about expeditions to Antarctica — old and new
- Identify ways of crossing ice by dog sled, skis and motorised sleigh

Science

- Discuss how people and animals keep warm in very cold places
- Show freezing and thawing with ice cubes and ice crystals
- Retell the life cycle of penguins
- Discuss or make a frieze which compares life-forms in polar regions
- Compare life in a penguin colony with another bird colony

Language

- Retell the story in own words and add other adventures
- Discuss hopes and fears in the story
- Imagine what it might feel like to be different penguins in the story
- Write a day in the life of another creature in the Antarctic
- Gather words and phrases which describe the landscape, light and seasons

- Role-play the story of making a journey across Antarctica

Little boat (Henderson 1995)

Geography

- Compare memories and pictures of the seaside
- Locate any seaside visits on a map
- Plan an imaginary visit to the seaside
- Compare different types of boats and people's work on or by the sea
- Use pictures to identify vocabulary associated with shore and sea
- Chart the journey of the little boat

Science

- Design and test a model boat using different materials
- Model a beach using sand tray, water and a hairdryer
- Discuss beach safety, currents and tidal movement
- Compare rough and smooth stones and pebbles
- Experiment with floating and sinking different objects
- Discuss rubbish on beaches and the dangers it poses to life forms
- Compare rock pools and the ocean floor
- Discuss lighthouses and send messages to each other using mirrors/torches
- Identify how clouds link with different kinds of weather conditions

Language

- Retell the story from the little boat's point of view
- Role-play a day's visit to the seaside
- Gather words and phrases about the sea and light on water
- Imagine a day working on an oil rig, ocean liner, fishing boat, lifeboat or in a beach cafe
- Write about something special you have lost or found
- Describe one part of the story in detail
- Devise a code of safe practice for any situation in the story

Through my window (Bradman and Browne 1989)

Geography

- Compare scenes and windows from home and school
- Discuss street scenes in different places
- Plan, sequence and record a local journey
- Identify different types of work and deliveries
- Interview someone who works in the school
- Model the flat or estate in the story
- Identify housing types and designs
- Survey a local residential area
- Compare being unwell in different places

History

- Record old and new features in a local area
- Compare types of work in the home — now and then
- Research medical care and being unwell — now and then
- Compare street sounds and scenes — old and new
- Make a memory box
- Compare home life — now and then
- Compare home delivery services — now and then
- Interview an older person about their childhood memories

Maths

- Devise a timetable for a day at home
- Timetable busy and quiet periods on the estate or in school or local area
- Count and classify features you can see in the local vicinity
- Compare timetables for a person at work in the story and one at school
- Calculate numbers of windows around school and at home

Babylon (Paton Walsh 1992)

Geography

- Compare story setting with local vicity
- Identify transport routes and features in local vicinity — old and new
- Survey local environment for litter, junk and graffiti
- Discuss how places change during different seasons
- Identify wild and cultivated areas within school grounds or local area
- Write to the Jamaican or a West African Tourist Board and make a display
- Invite a local planner to talk about the local area and community
- Invite someone to talk about times spent in or memories of another country
- Discuss the need for shelter and how people's homes vary
- Survey a local food shop or market and identify origins of produce
- Make a class survey of food eaten by the class

History

- Compare story setting and local area — now and then
- Make a timeline for the story setting — What came first?
- Gather memories of how places change over time
- Find out if your local area has links with other countries — old and new
- Explore links between West Africa, the Caribbean and your own locality
- Find out about the Hanging Gardens of Babylon and compare with story
- Locate Babylon and other wonders of the ancient world on a globe
- Make a memory box or paper patchwork quilt of memories
- Trace the history of canals and railways in your area

Language

- Collect words and sayings from Jamaica, West Africa and local area
- Encourage creative writing about memories and feelings of displacement
- Discuss the need for shelter and the problems of having no home
- Find out what 'By the waters of Babylon' means
- Collect other songs which contain clues or stories about the past
- Discuss how and why families move into and away from different places
- Plan how the class might welcome a new family into the area
- Plan a Caribbean meal and devise a menu card
- Write creatively about a very special place

Maths

- Use railway timetables
- Survey homes, gardens and shops in local area
- Make a survey of family connections with other places
- Calculate time differences and currency values
- Calculate distances between places mentioned in story
- Survey local shopping routes and choose a site for locating recycling facilties

Science

- Compare food preservation techniques from different countreis
- Design a bridge or viaduct and test for strength
- Test growing conditions and growth rates for seeds
- Survey how light is reflected indoors and outside
- Survey for pollution, moisture, etc., indicators
- Devise a Green policy or wildlife area for the school
- Devise a system for watering plants, which can move move water uphill

Grandfather's pencil and the room of stories (Foreman 1995)

Geography

- Compare homes, towns and views seen from a school or bedroom window with the pictures in story
- Locate forests and oceans using a globe and atlas
- Chart and compare the different journeys in the story
- Sequence pictures of places passed on the different journeys
- Survey journeys made by class
- Compare different modes of transport and reasons for journeys

History

- Survey the local area for evidence of continuity and change
- Compare design of clothes, toys and shops — old and new
- Compare bridge scenes and townscape — continuity and change
- Make a timeline for characters in the story
- Gather materials for a display about childhood memories

Science

- Experiment with floating and sinking different objects
- Model wind movements over water using hair-dryer and water tray
- Discuss protection of wildlife in forests and in local area
- Find out about which animals make simple tools
- Design and test simple tools using 'scrap' materials
- Design and build a bridge using different materials

Maths

- Compare distances of travelling by different forms of transport
- Survey traffic flows in local area
- Make a scale model of buildings shown in the story
- Calculate how much it would cost to carpet a bedroom

Language

- Tell the story of the whale button
- Discuss why people hunt whales — now and in the past
- Discuss and write about the journeys of other items found in the story
- Imagine that an object at home or school could share its memories
- Design an estate agent's brochure for a house — old or new
- Making a class survey of dreams
- Retell a dream
- Find out about what kind of things other people have said about dreams and memories

Appendix 1: Information sources for children's books

The Africa Centre, 38 King Street, Covent Garden, London WC2E 8JT.
Telephone 0171 836 1973

Book Trust Scotland, The Scottish Book Centre, Fountainbridge Library, 137 Dundee Street, Edinburgh EH11 1BG.
Telephone 0131 229 3663

Books for Keeps, 6 Brightfield Road, Lee, London SE12 8QF. Publisher of *The Green Guide to Children's Books*, Hill, R. (ed.) (1992), ISBN 1 87156 601 0.

Books for your children magazine, 49 High Street, Henley-in-Arden, West Midlands B95 5AA

Centre for Global Education, University of York, Heslington, York YO1 5DD.
Telephone 01904 433444

Children's Book Foundation, Book Trust, 45 East Hill, London SW13 2QZ.
Telephone 0181 870 9055

The Children's Bookshop, Lindley, Huddersfield, West Yorkshire HD3 3JF.
Telephone 01484 658013

The Commonwealth Institute, Kensington High Street, London W8 6NQ.
Telephone 0171 603 4535

Development Education Association, 29-31 Cowper Street, London EC2A 4AP.
Telephone 0171 490 8108

Development Education Dispatch Unit, 153 Cardigan Road, Leeds LS6 1LJ.
Telephone 0113 278 4030

British Section International Board on Books for Young People, c/o Child Literature Research Centre, Roehampton Institute, Downshire House, Roehampton Lane, London SW15 4HT. Telephone 0181 392 3346

Humanities Education Centre, Tower Hamlets Professional Development Centre, English Street, London E3 4TA.
Telephone 0181 981 0183

Letterbox Library, 2nd Floor, Leroy House, 436 Essex Road, London N1 3QP.
Telephone 0171 226 1633

National Library for the Handicapped Child, Wellington House, Wellington Road, Reading, Berkshire RG11 2AG.
Telephone 01734 891101

The Poetry Library, Children's Section, Royal Festival Hall, Belvedere Road, London SE1 8XZ.
Telephone 0171 226 1633

Reading and Language Information Centre, University of Reading, Bulmershe Court, Earley, Reading, Berkshire RG6 1HY.
Telephone 01734 318820

Appendix 2: Bibliography

References

Abse, D. (1992)
There was a young man from Cardiff,
Penguin (ISBN 0 14 015668 2)

Appiah, P. (1987)
Tales of an Ashanti father (Ghana),
André Deutsch (ISBN 0 233 98126 8)

Benjamin, F. (1995)
Coming to England,
Pavilion Books (ISBN 1 85793 154 8)

Bradman, T. and Browne, E. (1989)
Through my window,
Mammoth (ISBN 0 7497 0161 7)

Chapple, S. (ed.) (1989)
Becoming a writer,
National Writing Project/Thomas Nelson
(ISBN 0 17 424113 5)

Colledge, C. (1984)
Classroom photography,
Ilford Photographic

Curriculum Council for Wales (1991)
Geography in the National Curriculum: non-statutory guidance for teachers, pages 5–6,
Curriculum Council for Wales

Daly, N (1993)
Not so fast, Songololo!,
Picture Puffin (ISBN 0 14 050715 9)

Department for Education (1995)
Geography in the National Curriculum,
HMSO (ISBN 0 11 270886 2)

Foreman, M. (1995)
Grandfather's pencil and the room of stories,
Red Fox (ISBN 0 09 950331 X)

Gavin J. (1989)
The magic orange tree and other Haitian folk tales (ed. Wolkstein, D.),
Schocken, NY (ISBN 0 8052 0650 7)

Gergahty, P. (1995)
Solo,
Random House (ISBN 0 09 176733 4)

Gray, N. and Ray, J. (1991)
A balloon for Granddad,
Orchard Books (ISBN 1 85213 652 9)

Grifalconi, A. (1989)
The village of round and square houses,
Macmillan (ISBN 0 3334 8521 1)

Grimm, J. and Grimm, W. (1986)
The elves and the shoemaker,
North-South Books (ISBN 0 200728 80 6)

Harbott, I. and Harbott, G. (1990)
The farmer's gift,
André Deutsch (ISBN 0 233 98486 0).

Hathorn, L. (1994)
Way home,
Anderson Press (ISBN 0 86264 541 7)

Hedderwick, M. (1989)
Katie Morag and the tiresome teddy,
Collins (ISBN 0 00 663161 4)

Henderson, K. (1995)
Little boat,
Walker Books (ISBN 0 7445 2181 5)

Hughes, J. and Marsden, B. (1995)
'Revising courses at key stage 2',
Primary Geographer, No. 21, pp. 15-17

Hughes, S. (1993) 'Grandma's pictures', from
The big Alfie and Annie Rose storybook,
Red Fox (0 09 975030 9)

Hughes, S. (1988)
When we went to the park,
Walker Books (ISBN 0 7445 0301 9)

Isadora, R. (1992)
Over the green hills,
Red Fox (ISBN 0 09 926541 9)

Jonas, A. (1992)
The quilt,
Walker Books (ISBN 0 7445 2381 8)

Kingsley, M.H. (1993)
Travels in West Africa (ed. Huxley, E.),
Everyman (ISBN 0 460 87394 6)

Kirollos, S. (ed.) (1989)
The wind children and other tales from Japan,
André Deutsch (ISBN 0 233 98408 9)

Lee, L. (1970)
Cider with Rosie,
Penguin (ISBN 0 14 001682 1)

Lewis, C.S. (1993)
The Chronicles of Narnia: the lion, the witch and the wardrobe,
HarperCollins, (ISBN 0 00 671663 6)

Mais, S.P.B. (1938)
Delight in books,
A. Wheaton and Co.

Marshall, J.V. (1979)
Walkabout
Puffin

Norris Nicholson, H. (1993)
Inspirations for geography,
Scholastic (ISBN 0 590 53046 1)

Paton Walsh, J. (1992)
Babylon,
Red Fox (ISBN 0 09 938080 3)

Prater, J. (1993)
Can't catch me,
Picture Puffin (ISBN 0 14 050526 1)

Southall, I. (1967)
Ash Road,
Puffin

Spier, P. (1990)
Tin Lizzie and little Nell,
Doubleday (ISBN 0 385 09470 1)

Other suitable stories

Armitage, R. and Armitage, D. (1993)
The lighthouse keeper's rescue,
Picture Puffin (ISBN 0 14 054185 3)

Atkinson, E. (1995)
Greyfriar's Bobby,
Anderson Press (ISBN 0 86264 571 9)

Baker, J. (1992)
Where the forest meets the sea,
Walker Books (ISBN 0 7445 1305 7)

Brett, J. (1995)
Town mouse, country mouse,
Hamish Hamilton (ISBN 0 241 13537 0)

Cameron, A. (1993)
The most beautiful place in the world,
Young Corgi (ISBN 0 5525 2601 0)

Dahl, R. (1993)
Fantastic Mr Fox,
Young Puffin (ISBN 0 14 032671 5)

Desai, A. (1989)
The village by the sea,
Penguin (ISBN 0 14 011886 1)

Ekwensi, C. (1991)
Drummer boy,
Heinemann, Kenya (ISBN 9966 46 412 3)

Flindall, J. (1990)
The journey home,
Walker Books (ISBN 0 7445 1461 4)

Foreman, M. (1974)
Dinosaurs and all that rubbish,
Picture Puffin (ISBN 0 14 055260 X)

French, F. (1994)
Little Inchkin,
Frances Lincoln (ISBN 0 7112 0917 0)

Ganly, H. (1986)
Jyoti's journey,
Andre Deutsch (ISBN 0233 97899 2)

Gates, S. (1993)
Deadline for Danny's beach,
Oxford University Press (ISBN 0 19 271696 4)

Hathorn, L. (1995)
Wonder thing,
Viking Penguin (ISBN 0 670 85328 3)

Hayes, R. (1989)
The fox in the wood. a wartime adventure,
Anglia Young Books (ISBN 1 871173 02 7)

Heide, F., Heide, P. and Gilliland, J.H. (1991)
The day of Ahmed's secret,
Gollancz (ISBN 0 575 05079 9)

Hicyilmac, G. (1990)
Against the storm,
Viking (ISBN 0 670 82960 9)

Hutchins, P. (1978)
Don't forget the bacon,
Picture Puffin (ISBN 0 14 050315 3)

Hutchins, P. (1992)
Rosie's walk,
Bodley Head (ISBN 0 370 00794 8)

Jacobs Altman, L. (1993)
Amelia's road,
Lee and Low (ISBN 0 880000 04 0)

Keeping, C. (1989)
Adam and Paradise island,
Oxford University Press (ISBN 0 19 279842 1)

Kroll, V. (1995)
Mâsai and I,
Puffin (ISBN 0 14 054833 5)

Loverseed, A. (1990)
Tikkatoo's journey,
Blackie (ISBN 0 216 92781 1)

Lutzeier, E. (1993)
Lost for words,
Oxford University Press (ISBN 0 19 271707 3)

McCrory, M. and Michael, E. (1989)
Grandmother's tale,
Magi (ISBN 1 85430 053 9)

Mennen, I. and Daly, N. (1990)
Somewhere in Africa,
Bodley Head (ISBN 0 744 52234 X)

Mollel, T.M. (1992)
Promise to the sun,
Brown Little (ISBN 0 316 88908 3)

Mollel, T.M. and Morin, P. (1993)
The orphan boy,
Oxford University Press (ISBN 0 19 540845 4)

Naidoo, B. (1987)
Journey to Jo'burg. A South African story,
Armada (ISBN 0 00 672693 3)

Naidoo, B. (1995)
Chain of fire,
Longman (ISBN 0 582 25403 5)

Rose, D.L. (1990)
The people who hugged the trees,
Roberts Rinehart (ISBN 0 9 119780 7)

Verma, A. (1986)
Bringing the rain to Kapiti Plain,
Picture Mac (ISBN 0 3333 5164 9)

Waddell, M. (1983)
Going west,
Andersen Press (ISBN 0 862 64052 0)

Wallace, K. (1993)
Think of an eel,
Walker Books (ISBN 0 7445 3639 1)

Westall, R. (1992)
Stormsearch,
Puffin (ISBN 0 14 34468 3)

Wilson, B.K. and Lessac, F. (1991)
Turtle and the islands,
F. Lincoln (ISBN 0 7112 0697 X)

Further reading

Brennan, F. *et al.* (1994)
Guidelines for good practice in development education,
Development Education Support Centre

Colwell, E. (1991)
Storytelling (second edition)
Faber and Faber (ISBN 0 903355 35 3)

Development Education Centre (Birmingham) (1994)
Long ago and far away: activities for using stories for history and geography at key stage 1,
DEC (Birmingham) (ISBN 0 948838 28 0)

DEC (Birmingham) (1991)
Start with a story: supporting young children's exploration of issues,
DEC (Birmingham) (ISBN 0 948838 20 5)

Humanities Education Centre (1996)
Storyworlds,
HEC, Tower Hamlets (ISBN 1 873928 58 0)

Lewis, E. (1994)
'Inside story: geography in children's books',
Primary Geographer (series of articles)

Lewis, E. and Watts, S. (1995)
'A world of words - primary geography and language development',
Primary Geographer, No. 21, pp. 33-35